Living My New Life

Living My New Life

Copyright © 2019 New Life Church

All rights reserved. Except as permitted under the U.S. Copyright Act of 1976, no part of this publication may be reproduced, distributed, or transmitted in any form or by any means, or stored in a database or retrieval system, without the prior written permission of the author.

Scripture quotations marked (HCSB) are taken from the Holman Christian Standard Bible®, Copyright © 1999, 2000, 2002, 2003, 2009, by Holman Bible Publishers. Used by permission.

Scripture quotations marked (KJV) are taken from The King James Version which is public domain.

Scripture quotations marked (MEV) are taken from the Modern English Version. Copyright © 2014 by Military Bible Association. Used by permission. All rights reserved.

Scripture quotations marked (MSG) are taken from The Message. Copyright © 1993, 1994, 1995, 1996, 2000, 2001, 2002. Used by permission of NavPress Publishing Group.

Scriptures quotations marked (NIV®) are taken from The Holy Bible, New International Version®, Copyright © 1973, 1978, 1984, 2011 by Biblica, Inc.® Used by permission. All rights reserved worldwide.

Scripture quotations marked (NKJV) are taken from the New King James Version®, Copyright © 1982 by Thomas Nelson. Used by permission. All rights reserved.

Scripture quotations marked (TPT) are from The Passion Translation®. Copyright © 2017, 2018 by Passion & Fire Ministries, Inc. Used by permission. All rights reserved. ThePassionTranslation.com

Author Sally H. Brazell

Co-Author Amy D. Maxwell

Cover Designer Carolynn C. Collins

Interior Designer Holly D. Murray

Editor Holly D. Murray

Table of Contents

Purpose 1

Love 3

Read 6

Pray 9

Listen 13

Connect 15

Worship 19

Share 23

Determine 26

A Personal Prayer 30

New Life Church 32

Purpose

Congratulations on making the best decision of your life!

I once heard it said that the two greatest days of your life are the day you are born and the day you know why. Living a life with purpose is really what we all want! Inside of each of us is the desire to make a difference, help others, do something great, and live a life of success. None of these things can be accomplished without having Jesus in our life. He is the one who makes the difference!

When we ask Jesus to come into our life and be our Lord and Savior, He is the key that unlocks all the promises of God. His message is this:

> If you confess with your mouth, "Jesus is Lord," and believe in your heart that God raised Him from the dead, *you will be saved*. One believes with the heart, resulting in righteousness, and one confesses with the mouth, resulting in salvation. Now the Scripture says, everyone who believes on Him will not be put to shame, for there is no distinction between Jew and Greek, since the same Lord of all is rich to all who call on Him. *For everyone who calls on the name of the Lord will be saved.* (Romans 10:9-13, HCSB)

What a hope-filled promise that is! The salvation Jesus offers is truly for every single person.

Not only is salvation available for everyone, but Jesus desires to build a relationship with us, as well! John 14:6 reads, "Jesus told him, 'I am the way, the truth, and the life. No one comes to the Father except through Me'" (HCSB). Meeting Jesus and developing a personal relationship with Him is what being a disciple is all about.

This book is designed to support you as you develop your relationship with Jesus, your Savior. As you read the next few pages, it is our desire to help you grow because today is the start of your *new life*! It is a new day. The old is gone, and now it's time to focus forward, know the *love* God has for you, and understand what life is all about.

Love

*"For God so loved the world that He gave
His one and only Son, that whoever believes in Him
shall not perish but have eternal life."*
John 3:16 NIV

In the beginning, God made the world. He created man, woman, and everything in the universe. Perfect and holy, God's plan was simple. He created man to have a relationship with Him for His glory.

Mankind experienced God's love without limitations or boundaries. He had complete access to God and His love. God's love was the core of all things, and it was perfect, good, and right. You can read about all of this in Genesis chapter one.

Unfortunately, we read in Genesis chapter 3 that man fell. Mankind, using the free will God gave him, *chose* to disobey. The moment man chose to disobey, sin came into the world. Man's perfect relationship with God was severed, and death, evil, and disease now inhabited the world. This separated us from God, our creator.

Romans 5:12 (TPT) states, "When Adam sinned, the entire world was affected. Sin entered the human experience, and death was the result. And so, death followed this sin, casting its shadow over all humanity, because all have sinned." Romans 3:23 (HCSB) reads, "For all have sinned and fall short of the glory of God."

Sin came in and corrupted this world and everything in it. And we do not have the power within ourselves to defeat sin. We need Jesus for that! Our attempts are futile and only confuse the situation and add to the chaos.

God knew we could not overcome sin solely by ourselves. There is good news, however, which we refer to as the Gospel! Jesus made it possible to renew our fellowship with God. He gave His life in our place.

Death was the condition of our disobedience, yet Jesus took the sins of the world upon Himself, who had no sin, and died on the cross for us all . . . for you and for me! He personally carried our sins in His body on the cross so that we can be dead to sin and live for what is right. What a gift! Ephesians 2:8-9 tells us the following:

> For it was only through this wonderful grace that we believed in Him. Nothing we did could ever earn this salvation, for it was the gracious gift from God that brought us to Christ. So no one will ever be able to boast, for salvation is never a reward for good works or human striving. (TPT)

It isn't based on our good works. Instead, the moment we ask Jesus into our hearts, we become a child of God, a new creation, and we belong to Him! This means that His eternal promises are ours and we have been set free from sin and death by the blood of Jesus Christ – which He shed on the cross when He died for us. How exciting!

This does not mean that life will now be perfect without problems. A perfect life happens in Heaven, which we have access to through Jesus when we asked Him into our hearts and where we will reside when we leave this world. Until then, we can remember that nothing can separate us from God's love unless we allow it to.

Romans 8:38a (TPT) reads, "So now I live with the confidence that there is nothing in the universe with the power to separate us from God's love." He will always be with us, always making things right. And if we remain in Him and in His love, all things are new!

When we make mistakes, we can go to Him and ask for forgiveness, and He will cleanse our heart and make it white as snow! Why? Because Jesus loves us!

1 John 1:9 reads, "If we confess our sins, He is faithful and just to forgive us our sins and to cleanse us from all unrighteousness" (KJV). Likewise, Isaiah 1:18 (KJV) confirms, "'Come now, let's settle this,' says the Lord. 'Though your sins are like scarlet, I will make them as white as snow. Though they are red like crimson, I will make them as white as wool.'"

This is just the beginning of your new journey and the greatest decision you have ever made. You are loved so much! He has made a way just for you, and you will not be disappointed!

Read

*"How can a young man stay pure?
Only by living in the Word of God and walking in its truth."
Psalm 119:9 TPT*

You may have several questions once you have asked Jesus into your heart. Your questions may include the following: What now? What's next? What does God want me to do?

God has not left us to figure all of this out on our own. Remember, He did all this to renew our fellowship with Him. God reveals Himself to us through His Word, the Bible, and uses it to shape our hearts and lives. Reading the Word of God is as vital to our spiritual growth as food is to our physical body. Matthew 4:4b (MSG) tells us, "It takes more than bread to stay alive. It takes a steady stream of words from God's mouth." You will find rest and truth in His Word, and as you spend more time reading the Bible, it will transform you and bring you closer to God.

You are full of power because the greater one lives in you now. It doesn't matter how bad your circumstances might look right now, there is not a circumstance in this world that the kingdom of God can't change. It will produce supernatural blessing for you in any situation. So, if you're facing natural impossibilities, find out what God says about them in His Book.

Fill your heart and your mouth with His words and walk in the light of them. Matthew 6:33 (TPT) admonishes us, "So above all, constantly chase after the realm of God's kingdom and the righteousness that proceeds from him. Then all these less important things will be given to you abundantly." Determine as never before to seek first the kingdom of God where all things are possible, and step into the abundant life of blessing He's prepared for you!

Things you should know about the Bible:

- **The Bible is God's true Word:** "Every Scripture has been written by the Holy Spirit, the breath of God. It will empower you by its instruction and correction, giving you the strength to take the right direction and lead you deeper into the path of godliness" (2 Timothy 3:16, TPT).

- **The Bible (the Word) is Living and Active:** "For we have the living Word of God, which is full of energy, and it pierces more sharply than a two-edged sword. It will even penetrate to the very core of our being where soul and spirit, bone and marrow meet! It interprets and reveals the true thoughts and secret motives of our hearts" (Hebrews 4:12, TPT).

As believers, we should read the Bible every day and set aside times to study it as well. To truly understand His Word, we must read it in context and through its entirety. I know that may seem overwhelming, but just take it step by step, verse by verse. Pray, and ask God to help you interpret the verse. Surround yourself with experienced believers and get their feedback on what you are reading. The point is to increase your understanding and access His promises that are for you in His Word.

More scriptures to help you grow:

- "Don't just listen to the Word of Truth and not respond to it, for that is the essence of self-deception. So always let his Word become like poetry written and fulfilled by your life!" (James 1:22, TPT).
- "What a God you are! Your path for me has been perfect! All your promises have proven true. What a secure shelter for all those who turn to hide themselves in you! You are the wrap-around God [a shield] giving grace to me" (Psalms 18:30, TPT).
- "All Scripture is inspired by God and is profitable for teaching, for rebuking, for correcting, for training in righteousness, so that the man of God may be complete, equipped for every good work" (2 Timothy 3:16-17, HCSB).

Pray

"You will answer me, God, I know You always will, like You always do as You listen with love to my every prayer."
Psalm 17:6 TPT

Prayer is simply talking to God! That's right! The Creator of the entire universe wants to talk to us, and we have access to Him anytime we want! It's that easy!

Just as all relationships prioritize communication, God's relationship with us is no different. The more we communicate with God, the more we will relate to Him. As our relationship with God grows, we will come to understand Him more and value what He has to say.

Philippians 4:6 reads, "Don't be pulled in different directions or worried about a thing. Be saturated in prayer throughout each day, offering your faith-filled requests before God with overflowing gratitude. Tell him every detail of your life" (TPT). Yes, God is into the details! He wants you to communicate with Him about every aspect of your life.

Verse seven of the same book and chapter reads, "then God's wonderful peace that transcends human understanding, *will make the answers known to you* through Jesus Christ" (Philippians 4:7, TPT). You can expect that communication with God will be a two-way street! You won't be praying to One who only wants to take your words in with no feedback in return. He wants to help you know the right decision to make in every area of your life. Proverbs 3:5-6 (TPT) reads, "Trust in the Lord completely, and do not rely on your own opinions. With all your heart rely on Him to guide you, and He will lead you in every decision you make."

Prayer, again, is simply talking with God. There is not an exact formula on how to talk with God, but there is a simple model that others have used that may help you. This basic formula for prayer is like the Lord's prayer that Jesus gave as an example of how to pray in Matthew 6:9-13. Here is the formula, easily remembered with the acronym **ACTS**.

- *Adoration* – expressing to God how great He is and how you love Him.

- *Confession* – admitting your sins and being accountable for disobeying Him so that you can be cleansed.

- *Thanksgiving* – thanking God for His grace and forgiveness in your life and expressing your appreciation for everything He has done for you.

- *Supplication* – asking God for help with the things in your life that need changing and praying for others.

It is important that we find time to pray each day. Prayer helps us develop our trust in God and trusting Him will bring us success!

More scriptures to help you grow:

- "Since we have this confidence, we can also have great boldness before Him, for if we present any request agreeable to His will, He will hear us" (1 John 5:14, TPT).
- "You will call to Me and come and pray to Me, and I will listen to you" (Jeremiah 29:12, HCSB).
- "Be cheerful no matter what; pray all the time; thank God no matter what happens. This is the way God wants you who belong to Christ Jesus to live" (1 Thessalonians 5:16-18, MSG).
- "Jesus explained, 'I am the Way, I am the Truth, and I am the Life. No one comes next to the Father except through *union with me*. To know me is to know my Father too'" (John 14:6, TPT).
- "Therefore pray in this manner: Our Father who is in Heaven, hallowed be Your name. Your kingdom come; Your will be done on earth, as it is in Heaven. Give us this day our daily bread. And forgive us our debts, as we forgive our debtors. And lead us not into temptation, but deliver us from evil. For Yours is the kingdom and the power and the glory forever. Amen" (Matthew 6:9-13, HCSB).

- "The next morning, Jesus got up long before daylight, left the house while it was dark, and made his way to a secluded place to give himself to prayer" (Mark 1:35, TPT).
- "But Jesus often slipped away from them and went into the wilderness to pray" (Luke 5:16, TPT).

Listen

*"My own sheep will hear My voice
and I know each one, and they will follow Me."*
John 10:27 TPT

As much as we must talk to God daily, we must also learn to listen. All of us have prayed and have wanted clear answers to our questions or requests. For the most part, God hardly ever responds exactly how we expect or think He would. That is why we must be intentional in listening to Him.

It was even said of Jesus that He made time to just be with God. Quiet time is positioning yourself to hear from God. It is a time in which we are solely focused on God. Prayer, reading the Bible, and worshipping can help to settle our hearts and get us in that position. You must determine for yourself when and where you can best hear God and connect with His Spirit.

Remember, God can use countless ways to talk to you. He may reveal Himself through other believers, worship, your circumstance, etc. We must just be willing and ready to listen. The more we listen, the more we will recognize His voice. Like prayer, make it a habit to listen to God every day.

More scriptures to help you grow:

- "Call to Me and I will answer you, and tell you [and even show you] great and mighty things, [things which have been confined and hidden], which you do not know and understand and cannot distinguish" (Jeremiah 33:3, AMP).
- "Do what you have learned and received and heard and seen in me, and the God of peace will be with you" (Philippians 4:9, HCSB).
- "Listen to my testimony: I cried to God in my distress and He answered me. He freed me from all my fears!" (Psalms 34:4, TPT).
- "Now I'll listen carefully for Your voice and wait to hear whatever You say. Let me hear Your promise of peace – the message every one of Your godly lovers longs to hear. Don't let us in our ignorance turn back from following You" (Psalms 85:8, TPT).
- "And whenever you turn to the right or to the left, your ears will hear this command behind you: 'This is the way. Walk in it'" (Isaiah 30:21, HCSB).
- "The next morning, Jesus got up long before daylight, left the house while it was dark, and made His way to a secluded place to give Himself to prayer" (Mark 1:35, TPT).
- "But Jesus often slipped away from them and went into the wilderness to pray" (Luke 5:16, TPT).

Connect

"Every believer was faithfully devoted to following the teachings of the apostles. Their hearts were mutually linked to one another, sharing communion and coming together regularly for prayer. A deep sense of holy awe swept over everyone, and the apostles performed many miraculous signs and wonders. All the believers were in fellowship as one body, and they shared with one another whatever they had."
Acts 2:42-44 TPT

Community is important. It's even more important in the family of God. Sharing life with others gives us much-needed strength and support.

We need other believers around us to encourage and teach us. The sense of a family-community connection is there when other believers pray and worship with us. It is *refreshing* to be able to share our journey with others, taking the time to really get to know one another so that we know how to encourage one another in our walk of faith.

In the book of Acts, we see the believers coming together and living in fellowship with one another. They lived in unity with Jesus and with each other. They came together to pray, read God's Word, and support each other through difficult times. They helped each other grow and live life better in Jesus. They loved one another and encouraged those around them to do good things.

That same sense of community and connection is still vital to believers now. God's plan for community is not just for us to participate to see what we can get out of it. Instead, He designed this family-community to be equally about what we can give and how we can serve.

We are all called to serve the "body of Christ." We are all part of the body, this fellowship of believers, and we all play an intricate part. All of us together make up the whole "body of Christ." We must care for one another. If one suffers, we all hurt.

You have a role in this community of believers, and you need to spend some time thinking about what that role may be. We can each use our time, talents, and abilities to serve one another. We can accomplish more and flourish when we serve together.

More scriptures to help you grow:

- "So the eye cannot say to the hand, 'I don't need you!' Or again, the head can't say to the feet, 'I don't need you!' But even more, those parts of the body that seem to be weaker are necessary. And those parts of the body that we think to be less honorable, we clothe these with greater honor, and our unpresentable parts have a better presentation. But our presentable parts have no need of clothing. Instead, God has put the body together, giving greater honor to the less honorable, so that there would be no division in the body, but that the members would have the same concern for each other. So if one member suffers, all the members suffer with it; if one member is honored, all the members rejoice with it. Now you are the body of Christ, and individual members of it. And God has placed these in the church: first apostles, second prophets, third teachers, next miracles, then gifts of healing, helping, managing, various kinds of languages. Are all apostles? Are all prophets? Are all teachers? Do all do miracles? Do all have gifts of healing? Do all speak in other languages? Do all interpret? But desire the greater gifts. And I will show you an even better way" (1 Corinthians 12:21-31, HCSB).

- "But instead we will remain strong and always sincere in our love as we express the truth. All our direction and ministries will flow from Christ and lead us deeper into Him, the anointed Head of His body, the church. For His 'body' has been formed in His image and is closely joined together and constantly connected as one. And every member has been given divine gifts to contribute to the growth of all; and as these gifts operate effectively throughout the whole body, we are built up and made perfect in love" (Ephesians 4:15-16, TPT).

- "As everyone has received a gift, even so serve one another with it, as good stewards of the manifold grace of God" (1 Peter 4:10, MEV).
- "Discover creative ways to encourage others and to motivate them toward acts of compassion, doing beautiful works as expressions of love" (Hebrews 10:24, TPT).

Worship

*"You are worthy, our Lord and God,
to receive glory, honor, and power, for You created all things,
and by Your plan they were created and exist."*
Revelations 4:11 TPT

We were made for worship! God's initial design for us was just that – worship. We were created to worship Him. But it is more than just playing or singing music, it is literally a lifestyle of recognizing the awesomeness and goodness of God as we go about our daily lives.

Though we do not need to be at a church for us to worship, we are called by God to gather together. Hebrews 10:25 helps us to understand that the more time passes, the more important it is for us to meet as a church body. Church is where true worship as a community of believers occurs. We can't limit ourselves to just a podcast or a small group. As important as it is to worship in our quiet time, it is also important to worship together as the body of Christ. There is an anointing and power that comes from worshipping together.

As we think about how much God loves us, it is easy to worship! Psalms 100 exhorts us:

> Lift up a great shout of joy to the Lord! Go ahead and do it – everyone, everywhere! As you serve Him, be glad and worship Him. Sing your way into His

presence with joy! And realize what this really means – we have the privilege of worshipping the Lord our God. For He is our Creator and we belong to Him. We are the people of His pleasure. You can pass through His open gates with the password of praise. Come right into His presence with thanksgiving. Come bring your thank offering to Him and affectionately bless His beautiful name! For the Lord is always good and ready to receive you. He's so loving that it will amaze you – so kind that it will astound you! And He is famous for His faithfulness toward all. Everyone knows our God can be trusted, for He keeps His promises to every generation! (TPT)

There are so many reasons to worship God! He loves you beyond measure.

God's will for us is that we should desire to worship Him, read His Word, and fellowship with other believers. As we learn more about Him and His character, we will become more assured than ever of His unfailing love and great plans for us. Worshipping Him and being part of a community of believers is what church is all about!

More scriptures to help you grow:

- "This is not the time to pull away and neglect meeting together, as some have formed the habit of doing. In fact, we should come together even more frequently, eager to

encourage and urge each other onward as we anticipate that day drawing" (Hebrews 10:25, TPT).
- "Give to the Lord the glory of His name; worship the Lord in holy splendor" (Psalms 29:2, MEV).
- "Come and be His 'living stones' who are continually being assembled into a sanctuary for God. For now you serve as holy priests, offering up spiritual sacrifices that He readily accepts through Jesus Christ. For it says in Scripture: Look! I lay a cornerstone in Zion, a chosen and priceless stone! And whoever believes in Him will certainly not be disappointed" (1 Peter 2:5-6, TPT).
- "In the human body there are many parts and organs, each with a unique function. And so it is in the body of Christ. For though we are many, we've all been mingled into one body in Christ. This means that we are all vitally joined to one another, with each contributing to the others. God's marvelous grace imparts to each one of us varying gifts and ministries that are uniquely ours. So if God has given you the grace-gift of prophecy, you must activate your gift by using the proportion of faith you have to prophesy. If your grace-gift is serving, then thrive in serving others well. If you have the grace-gift of teaching, then be actively teaching and training others. If you have the grace-gift of encouragement, then use it often to encourage others. If you have the grace-gift of giving to meet the needs of others, then may you prosper in your generosity without any fanfare. If you have the gift of leadership, be

passionate about your leadership. And if you have the gift of showing compassion, then flourish in the cheerful display of compassion" (Romans 12:4-8, TPT).
- "Let the message about the Messiah dwell richly among you, teaching and admonishing one another in all wisdom, and singing psalms, hymns, and spiritual songs, with gratitude in your hearts to God" (Colossians 3:16, HCSB).
- "They continued steadfastly in the apostles' teaching and fellowship, in the breaking of bread and in the prayers" (Acts 2:42, MEV).

Share

"Don't stop! Keep on singing! Make His name famous!
Tell everyone every day how wonderful He is.
Give them the good news of our great Savior.
Take the message of His glory and miracles to every nation.
Tell them about all the amazing things He has done."
Psalm 96:2-3 TPT

One of the first physical steps we should take as followers of Christ is to be baptized. Just like Jesus was baptized in water, we should also be baptized in water. Baptism is our public proclamation that we are followers of Christ. It is an illustration of how we identify with the death, burial, and resurrection of Jesus Christ.

Baptism is not one of the steps to salvation. We are not saved by our works. However, it is an important symbol of God's salvation in and through us.

Here is where things come full circle. We are called by God to share the Gospel of Jesus Christ with others. This is not a suggestion – it is a command. We are called to make disciples, followers of Christ. We do this by telling others about Jesus and what He has done in our lives.

The thought of sharing your faith with others may be a scary thought. It will help if you keep it simple! The following is a list of basic ideas to get you started:

- Live a life that is genuine and clearly for Jesus.
- Pray for those with whom you want to share the Gospel.
- Remember that only the Holy Spirit can open eyes and hearts to God's truth.
- Share your story and tell about the difference God has made in your life.
- Use simple words to explain the salvation message – that we are all sinners and in need of forgiveness.
- Do not expect results immediately.

Sharing about Jesus isn't complicated. Salvation isn't complicated either. Telling others that Jesus loves them and how He has made your life better demonstrates your love for what matters most to God – people.

More scriptures to help you grow:
- "That's what baptism into the life of Jesus means. When we are lowered into the water, it is like the burial of Jesus; when we are raised up out of the water, it is like the resurrection of Jesus. Each of us is raised into a light-filled world by our Father so that we can see where we're going in our new grace-sovereign country" (Romans 6:3-5, MSG).
- "When all the people were baptized, Jesus also was baptized. As He was praying, Heaven opened, and the Holy Spirit descended on Him in a physical appearance

like a dove. And a voice came from Heaven: You are My beloved Son. I take delight in You!" (Luke 3:21-22, HCSB).
- "Jesus, undeterred, went right ahead and gave His charge: 'God authorized and commanded Me to commission you: Go out and train everyone you meet, far and near, in this way of life, marking them by baptism in the threefold name: Father, Son, and Holy Spirit. Then instruct them in the practice of all I have commanded you'" (Matthew 28:18-19, MSG).
- "And He said to them, 'As you go into all the world, preach openly the wonderful news of the gospel to the entire human race!'" (Mark 16:15, TPT).
- "Go ahead and give God thanks for all the glorious things He has done! Go ahead and worship Him! Tell everyone about His wonders!" (Psalms 105:1, TPT).
- "But give reverent honor in your hearts to the Anointed One and treat Him as the holy Master of your lives. And if anyone asks about the hope living within you, always be ready to explain your faith" (1 Peter 3:15, TPT).
- "But you will receive power when the Holy Spirit has come on you, and you will be My witnesses in Jerusalem, in all Judea, and Samaria, and to the ends of the earth!" (Acts 1:8, HCSB).

Determine

"Stand firm, and you will win life."
Luke 21:19 NIV

From this day on, let's determine to follow God and live a life devoted to Him. Romans 12:1 (MSG) encourages us in the following way:
> So here's what I want you to do, God helping you: Take your everyday, ordinary life – your sleeping, eating, going-to-work, and walking-around life – and place it before God as an offering. Embracing what God does for you is the best thing you can do for Him.

Trust Him enough to give Him every aspect of you! You can make this powerful confession: "Lord, I give You me! I give You my life and my thoughts - 24/7! I give You every part of my heart, my skills, my talents, my good and my bad; my strengths and my weaknesses I give to You now. I hold nothing back."

You are destined to succeed! You were made to conquer every plan the enemy has for you. 1 John 4:4 says, "You are of God, little children, and have overcome them: because greater is He that is in you, than he that is in the world" (MEV).

Satan is the god of this world. Scripture tells us, "The god of this world has blinded the minds of those who do not believe, lest the light of the glorious gospel of Christ, who is the image of God, should shine on them" (2 Corinthians 4:4, MEV). It is Satan, our enemy, whose desire is to keep people from knowing the love of Jesus Christ and from walking in all the good plans God has for them. But thank God, *greater* is He who is in us than the god of this world!

Greater is He that is in us than Satan. God in us is greater than demons. God is greater than evil spirits. He's greater than sickness and disease. God is the greater one! God lives in me and He lives in you! He that is in you is greater than any force you may come against.

When God is in you, you are born again. Another way of saying that is that you are born of God. The things in our past no longer are held against us, but instead, He washes us clean; we become brand new! Scripture says, "Therefore, if anyone is in Christ, he is a new creation; old things have passed away, and look, new things have come" (2 Corinthians 5:17, HCSB). This verse means that when we are born again, our spirits have been recreated – that we are of God.

Sadly, many Christians don't know they are born of God. They don't realize that they have received eternal life (the life and nature of God). They think eternal life is something they are *going to have* when they get to Heaven. Many think they have simply received forgiveness of sins for now.

But when we know that the man on the inside, the real man, has been born again and is a new self in Christ Jesus and that we rule and reign over Satan, we get a better understanding of how we can live a victorious life here and now. It is time for believers to become "God-inside-us" minded. Too long we have been weakness-minded, sickness-minded, inferiority-complex-minded, and trouble-and-poverty-minded. We've talked about it and thought about it until a serious condition of doubt, unbelief, and spiritual failure has been created in the church.

    This psychology of unbelief has robbed us of a vibrant Christian faith. It has kept us from living the abundant life Jesus intended us to have. John 10:10b (KJV) reads, "I am come that they might have life, and that they might have it more abundantly."

    Think about the second half of 1 John 4:4 for just a moment. "*Greater is He that is in you* than he that is in the world" (MEV). Grasp that! You are of God. The same mighty Spirit who raised Christ from the dead dwells inside of you! It's no wonder the Bible says, "all things are possible to him who believes" (Mark 9:23b, NKJV). It is because the God with whom all things are possible lives in *us*!

    Have you believed Jesus is the Son of God? Have you acknowledged that He died for you? Have you asked Jesus to be the Lord of your life? If not, now is the right time to receive Jesus as Savior!

*"For God so loved the world, that He gave
His only begotten Son, that whosoever believeth in
Him should not perish, but have everlasting life."
John 3:16 KJV*

A Personal Prayer

Dear Heavenly Father,

    I come to You in the name of Jesus. Your Word says in John 6:37, "he who comes to Me I will never cast out." Your Word says this, God, so I know You won't cast me out. I know You take me in, and I thank you for that.

    You said in Romans 10:13, "For whosoever shall call upon the name of the Lord shall be saved." I am calling on Your name, so I know you have saved me now. You also said in Romans 10:9-11, "and what is God's 'living message?' It is the revelation of faith for salvation, which is the message that we preach. For if you publicly declare with your mouth that Jesus is Lord and believe in your heart that God raised Him from the dead, you will experience salvation. The heart that believes in Him receives the gift of the righteousness of God – and then the mouth gives thanks to salvation. For the Scriptures encourage us with these words: 'Everyone who believes in Him will never be disappointed.'"

    I believe in my heart that Jesus Christ is the Son of God. I believe that He was raised from the dead for my justification, and I confess Him now as my Lord.

    Because Your Word says in Romans 10:10, "For with the heart one believes unto righteousness" and I do believe with my heart. I have now become the righteousness of God in Christ, according to 2 Corinthians 5:21, and I am saved!

Signed _____

Date _____

References for A Personal Prayer:
John 6:37b (MEV)
Romans 10:13 (KJV)
Romans 10:9-11 (TPT)
Romans 10:10a (MEV)

New Life Church

New Life Church exists to help you discover who you are and why you were born. Founded on the belief that Jesus came so that people could experience life in all its fullness (John 10:10), the church's vision is to love God, serve people, teach the Word, and change the world. New Life has three campuses - two located in Augusta and Grovetown, Georgia; and one in North Augusta, South Carolina.

The lead and founding pastors, Bryan and Rhonda Matthews, would love to invite you to connect with New Life Church! The church website (www.newlifeeveryday.com) is teeming with information on ways to get connected and includes videos to help you grow in your new life. You can connect with us on YouTube (New Life Everyday) and on Facebook (facebook.com/loveserveteachchange). Follow us on Instagram and Twitter: @newlifeeveryday

Made in the
USA
Columbia, SC